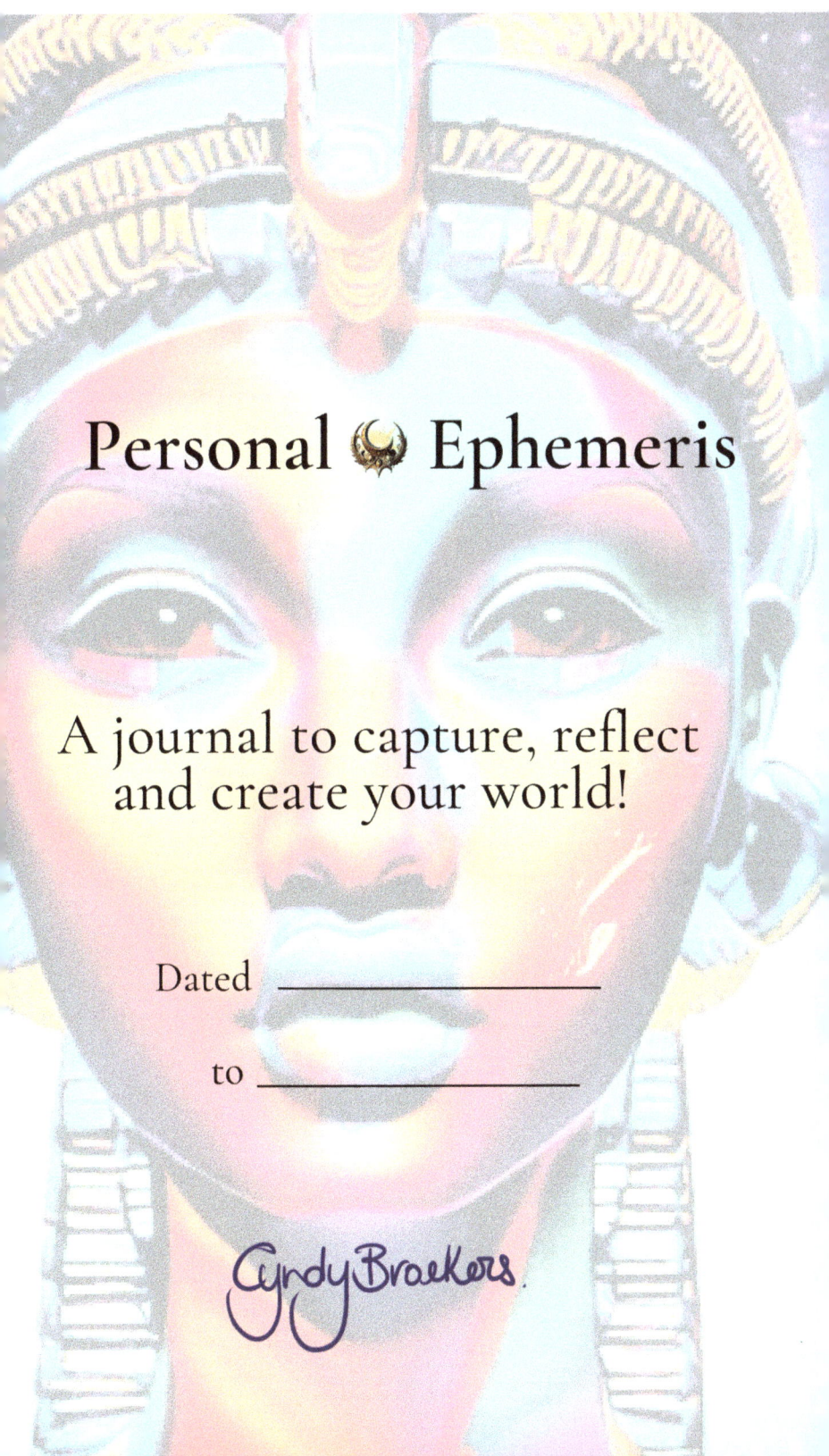

Personal 🌙 Ephemeris

A journal to capture, reflect and create your world!

Dated _____

to _____

Cyndy Brackers

Personal 🌙 Ephemeris is a work of my own creation.

The information in this book was correct at the time of publication, and the Author does not assume any liability for loss or damage caused by errors or omissions, again, this is my perspective, opinion, and experience, so it has been written as such.

Copyright @ 2023 by Cyndy Broekers

All rights reserved.

No part of this book may be reproduced or transmitted in any form or by any means, electronic or mechanical, including photocopying, recording, or by any information and retrieval systems, without the written permission of the Publisher, except where permitted by law.

ISBN - 978-1-961185-02-9

Cover, book design, images and layout by Cyndy Broekers,
cyndybroekers.com
(some images created using AI technology)

www.inomniaparatuspublishing.com

To creatives and powerful humans
who are reconnecting to their spark.

You are creating the change
you've been waiting for!

Why an ephemeris?

Your **Personal** 🌙 **Ephemeris** is a combination of diary, journal, productivity planner, sketchbook, to-do list, 'morning pages', goal tracker and so much more. It will become a record of your life that you can use to capture, reflect and grow.

An ephemeris is a reference book showing precisely when celestial phenomena occur. I recently discovered that a Greek translation of 'ephemeris' is diary or journal.

You, beautiful, are a celestial being - stardust - formed from galactic chemical evolution. You being here right now is due to a variety of phenomena that makes up your entire existence. It's exciting and electric!

As you use this book to record your day, plan your week, reflect on what's happened, ask yourself questions and build your self-awareness muscle, you'll be creating your very own personal ephemeris. It will remind you of what you're capable of. It will remind you of your light... **your spark!**

This image was created to represent my energetic blueprint ~ symbols of who I am, what I resonate with, my name and the work that I do.

Journalling has been a big part of my life and a great tool for self-reflection and seeking answers.

Today is the beginning of something special.

Seeking the magic combo

I'm an avid journaller (I still have a material bound journal that I received as a gift when I was 13 years old). I've tried so many types of journals, diaries, planners and at times juggled multiple hard copy and digital versions at once. I've been tweaking my own process for a few years now and I've created something that blends all of this together while keeping it flexible enough for you to make it truly your own!

Use your **Personal Ephemeris** to capture and record your day to day 'stuff'. Grab it when you need to pause, reflect on the week or month, gain valuable insights and set intentions for the coming days, week, month or year. Use it to house your inner most dreams and thoughts, to vent and think things through... to capture ideas and inspiration. You will make it completely yours!

There is more to you, waiting to be discovered. Waiting for you to reconnect to your spark! On the following pages I share how you can make the most of your journal. Let it evolve with you and go create your world!

The question you should be asking isn't,
'What do I want?'
or
'What are my goals?'
but
'What would excite me?'
- Tim Ferris

The Gift

How do you know how far you've come in your journey unless you're looking back and reflecting on *accurate* info? We humans are a funny bunch and when we want to remember something that happened a few months or weeks ago (let alone yesterday!), it can sometimes get a bit fuzzy.

That's where using a journal to capture it all can be really helpful.

There are deep gifts to be discovered in taking the time to journal.

It's in the simplest things where big shifts happen. Remember to record the seemingly small things.

Take time each week to reflect on the previous days and on what you have coming up. Look for patterns.

Knowing yourself inside and out builds self-trust and self-belief so you can stay focused and not be distracted or thrown off course by others.

Your life will evolve in unforeseen ways,
so stay open to the unexpected
- it's taking you exactly where you need to go.
- Unknown

A little about me

I'm a nostalgic artist and mentor. I love all things retro and I'm energetically driven to return to past experiences and memories, to support a deeper understanding of how life works, and to uncover clues to live out our unique blueprint and purpose.

I love bringing together the science of human behaviour, the esoteric and the grounded reality of being human to co-create a harmonious future. This is what I do for my clients which brings me so much joy.

One of my favourite things to do is show creatives how to reconnect to their spark, manage their time, develop sustainable habits, stretch their comfort zone and improve their relationship with uncertainty, so they can curate their world and achieve their creative goals and dreams.

When you reconnect to your spark, you start to notice patterns, possibilities and potential. Your whole world transforms. And this is my wish for you, through the use of this journal.

After a 30 year corporate career, beginning in Personnel and ending in Human Resources, I left that behind to discover more of what lights me up. I trained as a professional coach and Extended DISC consultant, helping entrepreneurs and small businesses as well as guiding one on one clients in their personal lives.

Along the way I've studied esoteric psychology, astrology, western herbal medicine, mythology, reiki and fine art. I've exhibited my artwork in group shows regularly for the past 3 years and won awards for some of my original paintings.

I've curated the frequency of my world by following clues that resonate with me; that light me up ~ which led me to help other creatives tap into their own unique magic.

I've created this journal to be used for your own personal use (or alongside my courses) so you can reconnect to your creative spark and truly believe in your potential. You'll start to remove and break down any old, unconscious patterns, making room for you to shine and create an amazing, rich, passionate life that you are meant to be living. Consistently.

How to make the most of this journal

Where to start? Anywhere you want! The beauty of this is you create your own structure, that works for you. Here are some ideas if you have Blank-Page-Stage-Fright:

🌙 Use the **ALL THE THINGS** pages to braindump everything that's in your head. Gather up all your to-do lists and tasks from your notes, emails, screenshots, calendars, ideas and pop in the most important ones here. There are 4 pages for this so you can continuously add to it. And you can create more throughout this journal.

🌙 **Intentions.** You might want to start the first journalling page with your intentions for this book.

🌙 **Free Writing.** This is good old fashioned long-form journalling, writing whatever comes to mind. It's a nice way to get things off your chest, out of your head and clear some space so you can focus for your day. What do you want to achieve? How do you want to use your time? How are you feeling today? What's been happening? What's on your plate right now?

🌙 **Monthly Pages.** You can use a fresh page or double page spread for the current month. I like to use the left side to record significant things that happened each day, so I'll write the dates down the left margin 1 - 31 with M-F next to each date and it's ready to populate. I'll use the right page as my monthly "to do" list (ie. what I need to, and want to achieve that month).

🌙 **Weekly Pages.** Every Sunday afternoon or evening, spend time going through your monthly task list (that right hand page I mentioned above), and the previous week to find any outstanding tasks. List the ones that you think you'll get to in the current week. Include appointments, lunch dates, birthdays and tasks.

🌙 **Daily Plan.** Add your events, appointments, birthdays, and tasks from your Weekly Spread. I like to start with the ONE thing that, if I accomplished it, I would be satisfied when I went to bed that night, even if nothing else got done. Then once I've jotted that down, I'll add 2 or 3 main tasks and any little things I can do that day.

🌙 **Evening Reflection.** You could use this journal at the end of your day to reflect; jot down any tasks, activities or events from the day. How you're feeling. What you're grateful for. And prep your tomorrow.

🌙 **Projects & Lists.** At any time, on any page, anywhere in this journal, you can start a list to capture ideas, inspiration, notes or tasks that relate to a project. The beauty of this (which I learned from Ryder Carroll's Bullet Journal method) is that you can continue adding to the project or list at any point in the journal - between daily, weekly and monthly pages; and between other lists and projects because of the Index.

🌙 **Index.** This is where the magic happens! I've learnt through experience that holding space for pages doesn't work. We over- or under-estimate what we need and end up with squished up notes or random blank pages throughout. So the index is here for you so you can start on the next blank page for whatever you're using your journal for in that moment; whether it's your daily to do list, morning pages, free writing, weekly plan, a project, quarterly goals, your record collection or a list of movies you want to watch. Then jot down that page in your Index with a good description. You'll be capturing information effectively and have an easy way to get back to it when you need to. At any time, on any page, anywhere!

For more resources on using this journal, visit cyndybroekers.com

INDEX

INDEX

INDEX

INDEX

Your energetic blueprint

The next three pages are spaces for you to include information about your energetic profiles. If you're familiar with astrology or human design and have a printed chart, you can stick a copy on these pages.

If you're familiar with your DISC profile, you can include that information too.

And I've got you covered if you don't have copies of these yet. Scan the QR code below to receive a free copy of each. When you're armed with information, you can go treasure hunting for valuable insights into the subtle energies that connect you to your spark.

If you can't scan the QR code, visit this page:
cyndybroekers.com/pages/my-blueprint

Your Astrological Chart

Scan the QR code below to receive your free astrological, human design and DISC charts.
Print them out and stick them in these pages to refer to as you create your awesome future!

If you can't scan the QR code, visit this page:
cyndybroekers.com/pages/my-blueprint

Your Human Design

Scan the QR code below to receive your free astrological, human design and DISC charts.
Print them out and stick them in these pages to refer to as you create your awesome future!

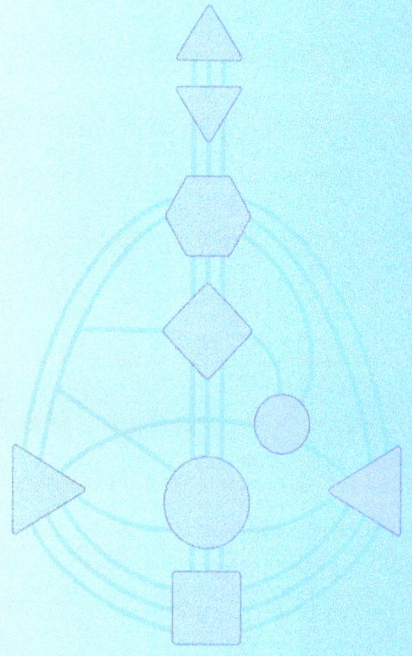

If you can't scan the QR code, visit this page:
cyndybroekers.com/pages/my-blueprint

Your DISC

Scan the QR code below to receive your free astrological, human design and DISC charts.
Print them out and stick them in these pages to refer to as you create your awesome future!

If you can't scan the QR code, visit this page:
cyndybroekers.com/pages/my-blueprint

ALL THE THINGS

ALL THE THINGS

ALL THE THINGS

ALL THE THINGS

The Future Is Waiting

original artwork by Cyndy Broekers

"In 20 years, you will be more disappointed by what you didn't do than by what you did." - Mark Twain

30

31

32

"Laugh my friend, for laugher ignites a fire within the pit of your belly and awakens your being." - Stella McCartney

40

"There is only one success. To be able to spend your life in your own way."
- Christopher Morley

48

49

50

52

"Who looks outside, dreams; who looks inside, awakens. - Carl Jung

56

"The privilege of a lifetime is being who you are." - Joseph Campbell

64

66

"To practice any art, no matter how well or badly,
is a way to make your soul grow. So do it. - Kurt Vonnegut

72

74

75

76

77

Love yourself a little bit more today.

80

84

"The beginning is always today."
- Mary Wollstonecraft

88

It's your birthright
to shine from your creative spark
and create the life you love.

original artwork by Cyndy Broekers

91

"They always say time changes things, but you actually have to change them yourself." - Andy Warhol

96

98

100

"Self esteem is seeing yourself as a flawed person, and still holding yourself in high regard." - Esther Perel

103

104

108

"The important thing is not to stop questioning.
Curiosity has its own reason for existing." - Albert Einstein

114

116

"It is our choices that show what we truly are, far more than our abilities." - JK Rowling

122

"Just as one candle lights another and can light thousands of other candles, so one heart illuminates another heart and can illuminate thousands of other hearts." - Tolstoy

130

132

133

Create a playlist that you can't help but dance to.
Play it as you get ready for your day to turbo boost your energy.

135

136

138

140

"You live but once; you might as well be amusing."
- Coco Chanel

144

148

149

"You are imperfect, you are wired for struggle, but you are worthy of love and belonging." - Brené Brown

154

155

"We must be the change we wish to see in our world."
- Mahatma Gandhi

160

162

163

165

"The one thing that can solve most of our problems is dancing."
- James Brown

168

172

173

"Out of your vulnerabilities will come your strength."
- Sigmund Freud

177

"They may forget what you said but they will never forget how you made them feel." - Carl W Buehner

184

186

"Every individual matters. Every individual has a role to play. Every individual makes a difference." - Jane Goodall

191

193

194

195

196

"Don't try to lessen yourself for the world; let the world catch up to you."
- Beyonce

200

201

202

203

204

205

"The question you should be asking isn't, 'What do I want?' or 'What are my goals?' but 'What would excite me?'" - Tim Ferris

208

209

212

www.ingramcontent.com/pod-product-compliance
Lightning Source LLC
Chambersburg PA
CBHW050733010526
44107CB00010B/831